AF256088

Spielplatz (Ort / Straße): _______________________________________

Tag der Überprüfung: _______________________________________

Name des Prüfers: _______________________________________

☐ Sichtkontrolle   ☐ Funktionskontrolle   ☐ Jährliche Hauptinspektion

Kontrollgegenstand	in Ordnung	Mängel

Mängel beseitigt		
Maßnahme	am	durch

Unterschrift des Vorgesetzten: _______________________

Spielplatz (Ort / Straße): _______________________________________

Tag der Überprüfung: _______________________________________

Name des Prüfers: _______________________________________

☐ Sichtkontrolle   ☐ Funktionskontrolle   ☐ Jährliche Hauptinspektion

Kontrollgegenstand	in Ordnung	Mängel

Mängel beseitigt		
Maßnahme	am	durch

Unterschrift des Vorgesetzten: _______________

Spielplatz (Ort / Straße): ______________________________________

Tag der Überprüfung: ______________________________________

Name des Prüfers: ______________________________________

☐ Sichtkontrolle ☐ Funktionskontrolle ☐ Jährliche Hauptinspektion

Kontrollgegenstand	in Ordnung	Mängel

Mängel beseitigt		
Maßnahme	am	durch

Unterschrift des Vorgesetzten: _______________

Spielplatz (Ort / Straße): _______________________________________

Tag der Überprüfung: _______________________________________

Name des Prüfers: _______________________________________

☐ Sichtkontrolle   ☐ Funktionskontrolle   ☐ Jährliche Hauptinspektion

Kontrollgegenstand	in Ordnung	Mängel

Mängel beseitigt		
Maßnahme	am	durch

Unterschrift des Vorgesetzten: _________________

Spielplatz (Ort / Straße): _______________________________________

Tag der Überprüfung: _______________________________________

Name des Prüfers: _______________________________________

☐ Sichtkontrolle ☐ Funktionskontrolle ☐ Jährliche Hauptinspektion

Kontrollgegenstand	in Ordnung	Mängel

Spielplatz (Ort / Straße): ____________________________

Tag der Überprüfung: ____________________________

Name des Prüfers: ____________________________

☐ Sichtkontrolle ☐ Funktionskontrolle ☐ Jährliche Hauptinspektion

Kontrollgegenstand	in Ordnung	Mängel

Mängel beseitigt		
Maßnahme	am	durch

Unterschrift des Vorgesetzten: _______________

Spielplatz (Ort / Straße): _______________________________

Tag der Überprüfung: _______________________________

Name des Prüfers: _______________________________

☐ Sichtkontrolle ☐ Funktionskontrolle ☐ Jährliche Hauptinspektio

Kontrollgegenstand	in Ordnung	Mängel

Mängel beseitigt		
Maßnahme	am	durch

Unterschrift des Vorgesetzten: _______________

Spielplatz (Ort / Straße): _______________________________

Tag der Überprüfung: _______________________________

Name des Prüfers: _______________________________

☐ Sichtkontrolle ☐ Funktionskontrolle ☐ Jährliche Hauptinspektion

Kontrollgegenstand	in Ordnung	Mängel

Mängel beseitigt		
Maßnahme	am	durch

Unterschrift des Vorgesetzten: ______________________

Spielplatz (Ort / Straße): _______________________________________

Tag der Überprüfung: _______________________________________

Name des Prüfers: _______________________________________

☐ Sichtkontrolle   ☐ Funktionskontrolle   ☐ Jährliche Hauptinspektion

Kontrollgegenstand	in Ordnung	Mängel

Mängel beseitigt		
Maßnahme	am	durch

Unterschrift des Vorgesetzten: _______________

Spielplatz (Ort / Straße): _______________________________________

Tag der Überprüfung: _______________________________________

Name des Prüfers: _______________________________________

☐ Sichtkontrolle   ☐ Funktionskontrolle   ☐ Jährliche Hauptinspektio

Kontrollgegenstand	in Ordnung	Mängel

Mängel beseitigt		
Maßnahme	am	durch

Unterschrift des Vorgesetzten: _____________________

Spielplatz (Ort / Straße): _______________________________________

Tag der Überprüfung: _______________________________________

Name des Prüfers: _______________________________________

☐ Sichtkontrolle　　☐ Funktionskontrolle　　☐ Jährliche Hauptinspektion

Kontrollgegenstand	in Ordnung	Mängel

Mängel beseitigt		
Maßnahme	**am**	**durch**

Unterschrift des Vorgesetzten: _______________

Spielplatz (Ort / Straße): _______________________________________

Tag der Überprüfung: _______________________________________

Name des Prüfers: _______________________________________

☐ Sichtkontrolle ☐ Funktionskontrolle ☐ Jährliche Hauptinspektion

Kontrollgegenstand	in Ordnung	Mängel

Mängel beseitigt		
Maßnahme	am	durch

Unterschrift des Vorgesetzten: _______________

Spielplatz (Ort / Straße): _______________________________

Tag der Überprüfung: _______________________________

Name des Prüfers: _______________________________

☐ Sichtkontrolle ☐ Funktionskontrolle ☐ Jährliche Hauptinspektion

Kontrollgegenstand	in Ordnung	Mängel

Mängel beseitigt		
Maßnahme	am	durch

Unterschrift des Vorgesetzten: _______________________

Spielplatz (Ort / Straße): _______________________________

Tag der Überprüfung: _______________________________

Name des Prüfers: _______________________________

☐ Sichtkontrolle   ☐ Funktionskontrolle   ☐ Jährliche Hauptinspektion

Kontrollgegenstand	in Ordnung	Mängel

Mängel beseitigt		
Maßnahme	am	durch

Unterschrift des Vorgesetzten: _________________

Spielplatz (Ort / Straße): _______________________

Tag der Überprüfung: _______________________

Name des Prüfers: _______________________

☐ Sichtkontrolle ☐ Funktionskontrolle ☐ Jährliche Hauptinspektion

Kontrollgegenstand	in Ordnung	Mängel

Mängel beseitigt		
Maßnahme	am	durch

Unterschrift des Vorgesetzten: _______________________

Spielplatz (Ort / Straße): _______________________________

Tag der Überprüfung: _______________________________

Name des Prüfers: _______________________________

☐ Sichtkontrolle ☐ Funktionskontrolle ☐ Jährliche Hauptinspektion

Kontrollgegenstand	in Ordnung	Mängel

Mängel beseitigt		
Maßnahme	am	durch

Unterschrift des Vorgesetzten: _________________

Spielplatz (Ort / Straße): _______________________________________

Tag der Überprüfung: _______________________________________

Name des Prüfers: _______________________________________

☐ Sichtkontrolle ☐ Funktionskontrolle ☐ Jährliche Hauptinspektion

Kontrollgegenstand	in Ordnung	Mängel

Mängel beseitigt		
Maßnahme	am	durch

Unterschrift des Vorgesetzten: _______________

Spielplatz (Ort / Straße): _______________________________________

Tag der Überprüfung: _______________________________________

Name des Prüfers: _______________________________________

☐ Sichtkontrolle   ☐ Funktionskontrolle   ☐ Jährliche Hauptinspektion

Kontrollgegenstand	in Ordnung	Mängel

Mängel beseitigt		
Maßnahme	am	durch

Unterschrift des Vorgesetzten: _______________

Spielplatz (Ort / Straße): _______________________________

Tag der Überprüfung: _______________________________

Name des Prüfers: _______________________________

☐ Sichtkontrolle ☐ Funktionskontrolle ☐ Jährliche Hauptinspektio

Kontrollgegenstand	in Ordnung	Mängel

Mängel beseitigt		
Maßnahme	am	durch

Unterschrift des Vorgesetzten: ______________________

Spielplatz (Ort / Straße): _______________________________

Tag der Überprüfung: _______________________________

Name des Prüfers: _______________________________

☐ Sichtkontrolle   ☐ Funktionskontrolle   ☐ Jährliche Hauptinspektion

Kontrollgegenstand	in Ordnung	Mängel

Mängel beseitigt		
Maßnahme	am	durch

Unterschrift des Vorgesetzten: _______________

Spielplatz (Ort / Straße): _______________________________________

Tag der Überprüfung: _______________________________________

Name des Prüfers: _______________________________________

☐ Sichtkontrolle   ☐ Funktionskontrolle   ☐ Jährliche Hauptinspektion

Kontrollgegenstand	in Ordnung	Mängel

Mängel beseitigt		
Maßnahme	am	durch

Unterschrift des Vorgesetzten: ________________________

Spielplatz (Ort / Straße): _______________________________

Tag der Überprüfung: _______________________________

Name des Prüfers: _______________________________

☐ Sichtkontrolle ☐ Funktionskontrolle ☐ Jährliche Hauptinspektio

Kontrollgegenstand	in Ordnung	Mängel

Mängel beseitigt		
Maßnahme	am	durch

Unterschrift des Vorgesetzten: _______________________

Spielplatz (Ort / Straße): _______________________________

Tag der Überprüfung: _______________________________

Name des Prüfers: _______________________________

☐ Sichtkontrolle ☐ Funktionskontrolle ☐ Jährliche Hauptinspektion

Kontrollgegenstand	in Ordnung	Mängel

Mängel beseitigt		
Maßnahme	am	durch

Unterschrift des Vorgesetzten: _______________________

Spielplatz (Ort / Straße): _______________________________

Tag der Überprüfung: _______________________________

Name des Prüfers: _______________________________

☐ Sichtkontrolle ☐ Funktionskontrolle ☐ Jährliche Hauptinspektion

Kontrollgegenstand	in Ordnung	Mängel

Mängel beseitigt		
Maßnahme	am	durch

Unterschrift des Vorgesetzten: _______________

Spielplatz (Ort / Straße): _______________________________

Tag der Überprüfung: _______________________________

Name des Prüfers: _______________________________

☐ Sichtkontrolle ☐ Funktionskontrolle ☐ Jährliche Hauptinspektio

Kontrollgegenstand	in Ordnung	Mängel

Mängel beseitigt

Maßnahme	am	durch

Unterschrift des Vorgesetzten: _______________

Spielplatz (Ort / Straße): _______________________________

Tag der Überprüfung: _______________________________

Name des Prüfers: _______________________________

☐ Sichtkontrolle ☐ Funktionskontrolle ☐ Jährliche Hauptinspektion

Kontrollgegenstand	in Ordnung	Mängel

Mängel beseitigt		
Maßnahme	am	durch

Unterschrift des Vorgesetzten: _______________________

Spielplatz (Ort / Straße): _______________________________________

Tag der Überprüfung: _______________________________________

Name des Prüfers: _______________________________________

☐ Sichtkontrolle   ☐ Funktionskontrolle   ☐ Jährliche Hauptinspektion

Kontrollgegenstand	in Ordnung	Mängel

Mängel beseitigt		
Maßnahme	am	durch

Unterschrift des Vorgesetzten: _____________________

Spielplatz (Ort / Straße): _______________________________________

Tag der Überprüfung: _______________________________________

Name des Prüfers: _______________________________________

☐ Sichtkontrolle ☐ Funktionskontrolle ☐ Jährliche Hauptinspektio

Kontrollgegenstand	in Ordnung	Mängel

Mängel beseitigt		
Maßnahme	am	durch

Unterschrift des Vorgesetzten: _____________________

Spielplatz (Ort / Straße): _________________________________

Tag der Überprüfung: _________________________________

Name des Prüfers: _________________________________

☐ Sichtkontrolle ☐ Funktionskontrolle ☐ Jährliche Hauptinspektion

Kontrollgegenstand	in Ordnung	Mängel

Mängel beseitigt		
Maßnahme	am	durch

Unterschrift des Vorgesetzten: _______________

Spielplatz (Ort / Straße): _______________________________

Tag der Überprüfung: _______________________________

Name des Prüfers: _______________________________

☐ Sichtkontrolle ☐ Funktionskontrolle ☐ Jährliche Hauptinspektion

Kontrollgegenstand	in Ordnung	Mängel

Mängel beseitigt		
Maßnahme	am	durch

Unterschrift des Vorgesetzten: _______________________

Spielplatz (Ort / Straße): _______________________

Tag der Überprüfung: _______________________

Name des Prüfers: _______________________

☐ Sichtkontrolle   ☐ Funktionskontrolle   ☐ Jährliche Hauptinspektio

Kontrollgegenstand	in Ordnung	Mängel

Mängel beseitigt		
Maßnahme	am	durch

Unterschrift des Vorgesetzten: _______________________

Spielplatz (Ort / Straße): _______________________________

Tag der Überprüfung: _______________________________

Name des Prüfers: _______________________________

☐ Sichtkontrolle ☐ Funktionskontrolle ☐ Jährliche Hauptinspektion

Kontrollgegenstand	in Ordnung	Mängel

Mängel beseitigt		
Maßnahme	am	durch

Unterschrift des Vorgesetzten: _________________

Spielplatz (Ort / Straße): _______________________________________

Tag der Überprüfung: _______________________________________

Name des Prüfers: _______________________________________

☐ Sichtkontrolle   ☐ Funktionskontrolle   ☐ Jährliche Hauptinspektion

Kontrollgegenstand	in Ordnung	Mängel

Mängel beseitigt		
Maßnahme	am	durch

Unterschrift des Vorgesetzten: _______________

Spielplatz (Ort / Straße): _______________________

Tag der Überprüfung: _______________________

Name des Prüfers: _______________________

☐ Sichtkontrolle ☐ Funktionskontrolle ☐ Jährliche Hauptinspektio

Kontrollgegenstand	in Ordnung	Mängel

Mängel beseitigt		
Maßnahme	am	durch

Unterschrift des Vorgesetzten: _______________

Spielplatz (Ort / Straße): ___________________________________

Tag der Überprüfung: _______________________________________

Name des Prüfers: ____

☐ Sichtkontrolle   ☐ Funktionskontrolle   ☐ Jährliche Hauptinspektion

Kontrollgegenstand	in Ordnung	Mängel

Mängel beseitigt		
Maßnahme	am	durch

Unterschrift des Vorgesetzten: _______________

Spielplatz (Ort / Straße): _______________________________________

Tag der Überprüfung: _______________________________________

Name des Prüfers: _______________________________________

☐ Sichtkontrolle ☐ Funktionskontrolle ☐ Jährliche Hauptinspektion

Kontrollgegenstand	in Ordnung	Mängel

Mängel beseitigt		
Maßnahme	am	durch

Unterschrift des Vorgesetzten: _______________________

Spielplatz (Ort / Straße): _______________________________

Tag der Überprüfung: _______________________________

Name des Prüfers: _______________________________

☐ Sichtkontrolle ☐ Funktionskontrolle ☐ Jährliche Hauptinspektio

Kontrollgegenstand	in Ordnung	Mängel

Mängel beseitigt		
Maßnahme	am	durch

Unterschrift des Vorgesetzten: _______________________

Spielplatz (Ort / Straße): _______________________________________

Tag der Überprüfung: _______________________________________

Name des Prüfers: _______________________________________

☐ Sichtkontrolle   ☐ Funktionskontrolle   ☐ Jährliche Hauptinspektion

Kontrollgegenstand	in Ordnung	Mängel

Mängel beseitigt		
Maßnahme	am	durch

Unterschrift des Vorgesetzten: ________________

Spielplatz (Ort / Straße): _______________________________________

Tag der Überprüfung: _______________________________________

Name des Prüfers: _______________________________________

☐ Sichtkontrolle ☐ Funktionskontrolle ☐ Jährliche Hauptinspektion

Kontrollgegenstand	in Ordnung	Mängel

Mängel beseitigt		
Maßnahme	am	durch

Unterschrift des Vorgesetzten: ______________________

Spielplatz (Ort / Straße): ___________________________________

Tag der Überprüfung: ___________________________________

Name des Prüfers: ___________________________________

☐ Sichtkontrolle   ☐ Funktionskontrolle   ☐ Jährliche Hauptinspektio

Kontrollgegenstand	in Ordnung	Mängel

Mängel beseitigt

Maßnahme	am	durch

Unterschrift des Vorgesetzten: _________________

Spielplatz (Ort / Straße): _______________________________

Tag der Überprüfung: _______________________________

Name des Prüfers: _______________________________

☐ Sichtkontrolle ☐ Funktionskontrolle ☐ Jährliche Hauptinspektion

Kontrollgegenstand	in Ordnung	Mängel

Mängel beseitigt		
Maßnahme	am	durch

Unterschrift des Vorgesetzten: _________________

Spielplatz (Ort / Straße): _______________________________________

Tag der Überprüfung: _______________________________________

Name des Prüfers: _______________________________________

☐ Sichtkontrolle ☐ Funktionskontrolle ☐ Jährliche Hauptinspektion

Kontrollgegenstand	in Ordnung	Mängel

Mängel beseitigt		
Maßnahme	am	durch

Unterschrift des Vorgesetzten: _______________

Spielplatz (Ort / Straße): _______________________________________

Tag der Überprüfung: _______________________________________

Name des Prüfers: _______________________________________

☐ Sichtkontrolle   ☐ Funktionskontrolle   ☐ Jährliche Hauptinspektion

Kontrollgegenstand	in Ordnung	Mängel

Mängel beseitigt		
Maßnahme	am	durch

Unterschrift des Vorgesetzten: _______________________

Spielplatz (Ort / Straße): _______________________________

Tag der Überprüfung: _______________________________

Name des Prüfers: _______________________________

☐ Sichtkontrolle ☐ Funktionskontrolle ☐ Jährliche Hauptinspektion

Kontrollgegenstand	in Ordnung	Mängel

Mängel beseitigt		
Maßnahme	am	durch

Unterschrift des Vorgesetzten: _______________

Spielplatz (Ort / Straße): _______________________________________

Tag der Überprüfung: _______________________________________

Name des Prüfers: _______________________________________

☐ Sichtkontrolle ☐ Funktionskontrolle ☐ Jährliche Hauptinspektion

Kontrollgegenstand	in Ordnung	Mängel

Mängel beseitigt		
Maßnahme	am	durch

Unterschrift des Vorgesetzten: _________________

Spielplatz (Ort / Straße): _______________________________

Tag der Überprüfung: _______________________________

Name des Prüfers: _______________________________

☐ Sichtkontrolle ☐ Funktionskontrolle ☐ Jährliche Hauptinspektio

Kontrollgegenstand	in Ordnung	Mängel

Mängel beseitigt		
Maßnahme	am	durch

Unterschrift des Vorgesetzten: _______________

Spielplatz (Ort / Straße): _______________________________

Tag der Überprüfung: _______________________________

Name des Prüfers: _______________________________

☐ Sichtkontrolle   ☐ Funktionskontrolle   ☐ Jährliche Hauptinspektion

Kontrollgegenstand	in Ordnung	Mängel

Mängel beseitigt		
Maßnahme	am	durch

Unterschrift des Vorgesetzten: _______________

Spielplatz (Ort / Straße): _______________________________________

Tag der Überprüfung: _______________________________________

Name des Prüfers: _______________________________________

☐ Sichtkontrolle ☐ Funktionskontrolle ☐ Jährliche Hauptinspektion

Kontrollgegenstand	in Ordnung	Mängel

Mängel beseitigt		
Maßnahme	am	durch

Unterschrift des Vorgesetzten: ______________________

Spielplatz (Ort / Straße): _______________________________

Tag der Überprüfung: _______________________________

Name des Prüfers: _______________________________

☐ Sichtkontrolle   ☐ Funktionskontrolle   ☐ Jährliche Hauptinspektio

Kontrollgegenstand	in Ordnung	Mängel

Mängel beseitigt		
Maßnahme	am	durch

Unterschrift des Vorgesetzten: ________________

Spielplatz (Ort / Straße): ___________________________________

Tag der Überprüfung: ___________________________________

Name des Prüfers: ___________________________________

☐ Sichtkontrolle ☐ Funktionskontrolle ☐ Jährliche Hauptinspektion

Kontrollgegenstand	in Ordnung	Mängel

Mängel beseitigt		
Maßnahme	am	durch

Unterschrift des Vorgesetzten: _______________

Spielplatz (Ort / Straße): _________________________________

Tag der Überprüfung: _________________________________

Name des Prüfers: _________________________________

☐ Sichtkontrolle ☐ Funktionskontrolle ☐ Jährliche Hauptinspektion

Kontrollgegenstand	in Ordnung	Mängel

Mängel beseitigt		
Maßnahme	am	durch

Unterschrift des Vorgesetzten: _______________

Spielplatz (Ort / Straße): _______________________________

Tag der Überprüfung: _______________________________

Name des Prüfers: _______________________________

☐ Sichtkontrolle ☐ Funktionskontrolle ☐ Jährliche Hauptinspektio

Kontrollgegenstand	in Ordnung	Mängel

Mängel beseitigt		
Maßnahme	am	durch

Unterschrift des Vorgesetzten: ___________________

Spielplatz (Ort / Straße): ______________________________

Tag der Überprüfung: ______________________________

Name des Prüfers: ______________________________

☐ Sichtkontrolle   ☐ Funktionskontrolle   ☐ Jährliche Hauptinspektion

Kontrollgegenstand	in Ordnung	Mängel

Mängel beseitigt		
Maßnahme	am	durch

Unterschrift des Vorgesetzten: _______________

Spielplatz (Ort / Straße): _______________________________________

Tag der Überprüfung: _______________________________________

Name des Prüfers: _______________________________________

☐ Sichtkontrolle ☐ Funktionskontrolle ☐ Jährliche Hauptinspektion

Kontrollgegenstand	in Ordnung	Mängel

Mängel beseitigt		
Maßnahme	am	durch

Unterschrift des Vorgesetzten: ________________________

Kontrollgegenstand	in Ordnung	Mängel

Mängel beseitigt		
Maßnahme	am	durch

Unterschrift des Vorgesetzten: ______________________

Spielplatz (Ort / Straße): _______________________________

Tag der Überprüfung: _______________________________

Name des Prüfers: _______________________________

☐ Sichtkontrolle ☐ Funktionskontrolle ☐ Jährliche Hauptinspektion

Kontrollgegenstand	in Ordnung	Mängel

Mängel beseitigt		
Maßnahme	am	durch

Unterschrift des Vorgesetzten: _______________

Spielplatz (Ort / Straße): _______________________________

Tag der Überprüfung: _______________________________

Name des Prüfers: _______________________________

☐ Sichtkontrolle ☐ Funktionskontrolle ☐ Jährliche Hauptinspektion

Kontrollgegenstand	in Ordnung	Mängel

Mängel beseitigt		
Maßnahme	am	durch

Unterschrift des Vorgesetzten: _______________________

Spielplatz (Ort / Straße): _______________________

Tag der Überprüfung: _______________________

Name des Prüfers: _______________________

☐ Sichtkontrolle   ☐ Funktionskontrolle   ☐ Jährliche Hauptinspektio

Kontrollgegenstand	in Ordnung	Mängel

Mängel beseitigt		
Maßnahme	am	durch

Unterschrift des Vorgesetzten: _______________

Spielplatz (Ort / Straße): _______________________________

Tag der Überprüfung: _______________________________

Name des Prüfers: _______________________________

☐ Sichtkontrolle ☐ Funktionskontrolle ☐ Jährliche Hauptinspektion

Kontrollgegenstand	in Ordnung	Mängel

Mängel beseitigt		
Maßnahme	am	durch

Unterschrift des Vorgesetzten: ______________________

www.ingramcontent.com/pod-product-compliance
Lightning Source LLC
Chambersburg PA
CBHW061541050726
47593CB00002B/860